Carolrhoda Books
A division of Lerner Publishing Group, Inc.
241 First Avenue North
Minneapolis, MN 55401 USA

For reading levels and more information, look up this
title at www.lernerbooks.com.

Library of Congress Cataloging-in-Publication Data

Hosford, Kate.
   [Poems. Selections]
   Feeding the flying Fanellis : and other poems from a Circus
chef / by Kate Hosford ; illustrated by Cosei Kawa.
      pages cm
   ISBN 978-1-4677-3905-4 (lib. bdg. : alk. paper)
   ISBN 978-1-4677-7511-3 (EB pdf)
      1. Cooks—Juvenile poetry. 2. Circus—Juvenile poetry. I. Kawa,
Cosei, illustrator. II. Title.
   PS3608.O77945A6 2015
   811'.6—dc23   2014011653

Manufactured in the United States of America
1 - VP - 7/15/15

To Chris, Charlie, and Andreas
—K.H.

To Towa
—C.K.

FEEDING THE FLYING FANELLIS

AND OTHER POEMS
FROM A CIRCUS CHEF

BY **KATE HOSFORD**
ILLUSTRATED BY **COSEI KAWA**

CAROLRHODA BOOKS • MINNEAPOLIS

IN THE CIRCUS KITCHEN

I've never turned a cartwheel, and I'm dizzy in high places.
I couldn't ever be a clown—I don't make funny faces.

But put me in the kitchen, and I think you'll be delighted.
Join us for a circus meal. Everyone's invited.

I handle special orders and unusual suggestions.
And if you have an allergy, just come to me with questions.

Put me in the kitchen, where the coffee's percolating.
I'll mash and melt with pleasure. I can't keep the circus waiting!

My days are long and sweaty, and the chaos never ends.
But still, I find I'm most content when cooking for my friends.

THE RINGMASTER

Our ringmaster never sits down for his meals.
With meetings, rehearsals, and crowds to impress,
I certainly know how our ringmaster feels,
Running around in a state of distress.

Inside of his hat is a picnic I made—
Salami and mustard, a mini-baguette,
Some hazelnut chocolates, and fresh lemonade.
My fabulous formula hasn't failed yet.

So when he is hungry for something to eat,
He knows it is hidden on top of his head.
This tasty selection that's also discreet
Is keeping our ringmaster properly fed.

THE HOMESICK STRONGMAN

The strongman joined us from Ukraine.
The tears fell down his face like rain.

I made him *vushka* and some tea
From his babushka's recipe.

He dried his eyes with one big hand.
"Thank you, Chef. You understand."

1

2

3

5

4

6

7

Рецепт

THE JUGGLER

Feeding this one is a struggle.
Why? Because he loves to juggle.

Anything that's slightly round
Will soon be far above the ground.

Buns at breakfast? Must avoid,
Grapes at dinner? I'm annoyed.

He's growing thin; his plate is bare.
All his food is in the air!

He doesn't even seem to care.
I think I'll feed him something square.

LITTLE BLUE

Little Blue jumps through his hoop
If I agree to cook him soup.

Chicken noodle, clam chowder,
Awful soup that's made from powder,

Cajun gumbo, callaloo.
It's really all the same to Blue.

But if he doesn't get his soup,
His perky ears will start to droop.

He'll trot across the circus ring,
Refusing to do anything.

His frantic trainer begs and pleads,
But Blue is clear about his needs.

He puts his nose up in the air.
He plants his feet. He doesn't care.

Even if the crowd is bored.
Or if his trainer feels ignored.

So in the end it's up to me
To cook his soup efficiently.

We serve the soup—he laps it up,
And soon he is a joyful pup.

Now he'll do a trick or two.
We've been well trained by Little Blue.

THE CONTORTIONIST TWINS

Twisty twins, from Paris, France,
Dressed in matching pairs of pants,
Tangled when they tried to dance,
And showtime's in an hour.

The twins are hardly overjoyed.
Colette says, "My career's destroyed!"
Annette says, "I'll be unemployed!"
The mood is turning sour.

"Oh, darling Chef," the twins both say.
"Will you help us, s'il vous plaît?"
I make their favorite, tarte flambée,
And hope they'll be less dour.

They smell the tarte; their knot unfurls.
Annette unwinds; Colette uncurls.
Soon I have two cheerful girls
And many pots to scour.

BORIS ON HIS TINY BIKE

An act that children really like
Is Boris on his tiny bike.

Boris is a giant guy.
The bike's eleven inches high.

I have to watch his food intake.
An extra bite—the bike could break!

MARTIN MCGARRIGLE

How does he manage it?
Martin McGarrigle—
Eating his oatmeal while
Walking on stilts.
Filled with such wonderful
Idiosyncrasy,
Dressing the animals
Up in his kilts.

THE TIGHTROPE WALKER

The tightrope walker is high-strung.
She climbs up to the highest rung

And orders up her balanced diet
In a voice that's far from quiet:

"Flounder and some new potatoes,
Garden lettuce and tomatoes,

"Twenty-seven grains of rice,
Avocado, just a slice!

"No caffeine or even tea.
Make sure that it's sugar-free.

"Nothing fried, nothing canned,
Processed foods are also banned.

"And make sure not to use the salt.
If I fall, it's all your fault!"

Perhaps she is a bit uptight.
Who wouldn't be, from such a height?

THE CLOWN

Sophisticated and polite,
Arriving first at every meal.
His conversations—pure delight!
This clown is really so genteel.

He's never once been coarse or rude
Like those who try to talk and chew.
But clowns must practice throwing food.
It's in his act—what can he do?

A pie lands daily in my face.
And still I find myself amused.
He begs my pardon with such grace
And asks if he can be excused.

Today he threw some custard pies
And turned our table upside down.
He knows it seems uncivilized,
But practice makes a perfect clown.

THE LION

The lion is a true gourmet
Who thinks about his food all day.

He smiles, flashing his incisors,
Just before the appetizers.

First comes antelope pâté,
Followed by a consommé.

His entrée is a wild boar.
He wolfs it down and roars for more.

He eats grilled warthog with his claws.
He tears through python with his jaws.

Now he's hunting for dessert.
He's started nibbling on my shirt!

I give him ostrich à la mode,
Topped with candied pygmy toad.

He licks his lips and starts to roar.
I hide behind the kitchen door.

"Would you like your cheese plate now?"
But all the lion does is growl.

The food is gone, but he's still here.
He's ravenous—that much is clear.

This beast will make me cook all night
To satisfy his appetite!

THE HUMAN CANNONBALL

When Hugo joined us, he was small.
He made a perfect cannonball.

They'd stick him in—he'd fly right out.
The audience would scream and shout.

But as he grew, he wanted snacks:
Pancakes piled in giant stacks,

Lovely cookies by the pound,
Yummy pastries by the mound.

Into the cannon he was squeezed,
His adolescent arms and knees.

The clown prepared him to be fired,
But Hugo felt quite uninspired.

"I'm bored with flying every night.
This cannon's getting rather tight.

I could be eating chocolate mousse.
Please, Chef, try to pry me loose."

He ate the mousse and several pies.
He ate the coconut surprise.

"And now," he said, "It wouldn't hurt
To have a little more dessert!"

I've tried him on a new regime
Of kale soufflé and broccoli cream.

"But Chef," he said, "why would I eat
A food that isn't even sweet?"

I might have played a part, I fear,
In compromising his career.

Is it a problem, after all,
To cater to this cannonball?

THE FLYING FANELLIS

Certainly, you've heard
About the fabulous Fanellis.
They only ask for lemon cakes
To fill their fearless bellies.

Mia has such energy.
She's soaring toward the sky.
And Papa's singing opera.
They're on a sugar high!

Mama flies toward Theo now.
She's speeding far too fast.
Theo barely grabs her hands
Before she whizzes past.

I know this flying fantasy
Could change in just a flash.
Unless this family gets a grip,
They'll have a sugar crash!

THE ONE AND ONLY GORGEOUS LENA

The one and only Gorgeous Lena,
Moscow's prima ballerina,

Found out that she had a knack
For dancing on a horse's back.

The horse, whose name is Mr. Redding,
Waits while Lena's pirouetting.

Mr. Redding, when he's able,
Joins her at the dinner table.

Often it's a hearty meal
Of carrots, oats, and apple peel.

Dessert is sugar cubes, of course—
Just perfect for a girl and horse.

Angeline

Our bravest beauty, Angeline,
Eats breakfast on the trampoline.
This acrobat (whose form is great!)
Makes sure the food stays on her plate.

Soaring, swooping—full of grace,
An artist with an angel's face.

The warm and witty Angeline
Is quite the somersaulting queen.
I'll share the secret to her bounces:
Milk shakes—always sixteen ounces.

Flipping, flying—watch her go!
Seven twisters in a row!

The long and limber Angeline
Will eat until her plate is clean.
I toss her omelets and knishes—
Anything that Angie wishes.

I think sweet Angie might have guessed
That she's the one I like the best.

THE FIRE-EATER

Avoid the Flaming Chili Sauce of Miss Miranda May.
She offers it to everyone, no matter what I say.

The lion tried it on his lunch and soon began to sway.
When Mr. Redding drank a drop, he found he couldn't neigh.
Then Lena simply smelled the sauce and fell into the hay.

But our fire-eater has to have her chilies every day.
She's heading toward my dinner now, much to my dismay.
This very harmful condiment is hardly child's play.

Even just the sight of it can take my breath away.
Avoid the Flaming Chili Sauce of Miss Miranda May!

HUGO BECOMES A PASTRY CHEF

I found poor Hugo sniffling while nibbling on a tart.
"My job," he said, "is not for someone capable and smart.

"I'm sick of satin underpants and flying through the air.
I hate this stupid little cape I always have to wear.

"Worst of all, the cannon is enough to make me deaf!
Couldn't this old cannonball become a pastry chef?"

Now Hugo's learning rapidly to run the pastry station.
If he continues to improve, I'll take my first vacation.

Today he made a layer cake and cherries jubilee.
"Chef," he said, "I didn't know how sweet my life could be!"

OUR SUMMER CIRCUS FEAST

For several days, we've hardly slept.
We've peeled and pickled, pared and prepped.
We've cooked so many sides and soups,
While drizzling sauce in loop-de-loops.

Our lovely Angie wants to eat
A loaf of bread from summer wheat.
Our clown would like some custard pies,
And Boris wants some tiny fries.

Our fire-eater has agreed
There really isn't any need
To share her hot sauce at our meal.
Instead, we'll give her flaming eel.

And finally, for the Fanellis,
Lemon cakes to fill their bellies;
Lobster bisque for Little Blue;
And for the lion, beef fondue.

Our other friends will be surprised
By dishes that we've both devised.
We hope they'll love what we invent.
Until we know, we're not content.

Our stove is hot; our pans are greased.
Our list of entrees has increased.
We'll have ten courses at the least—
Enjoy our summer circus feast!